The Taylor Brand

The Taylor / Lewis Family History From The Early '20s to Present

by

Mary Langford

authorHOUSE®

AuthorHouse™
1663 Liberty Drive, Suite 200
Bloomington, IN 47403
www.authorhouse.com
Phone: 1-800-839-8640

First published by AuthorHouse 11/29/2007

ISBN: 978-1-4343-5333-7 (sc)
ISBN: 978-1-4343-5334-4 (hc)

Printed in the United States of America
Bloomington, Indiana

This book is printed on acid-free paper.

The Taylor Brand
The Taylor / Lewis Family History From The Early '20s to Present

By
Mary Langford

Table of Contents

Dedication

I dedicate this book to the four surviving Taylor siblings,

Marie Taylor,

Gatisy Taylor-Edney,

L T Taylor

and

Vivian Taylor-Jones,

and to all the children,

grandchildren,

great-grandchildren

and

great, great, great - grandchildren

of the Taylor / Lewis family.

Acknowledgements

A special thanks to my daughter Virna Campbell-Langford for her constant urging me to document my family history. Many thanks to Vivian Taylor-Jones, Marie Taylor, Gatisy Taylor-Edney, and L T Taylor for my numerous long telephone calls. Also thanks to Eunice Faye Taylor-Dunda, Ira Lee Taylor-Austin-Evans, Marilyn Evans-Dixon, Gloria Jean Roney's 1968 Year-Book, Bessie Q. Taylor, James Phillip Austin, Cora Gilstrap Rankins, Clay Taylor's Holy Bible, and my many pictures and documents. Thanks again to Virna for typing the first draft and creating a disc. Also a special thanks to Langford for his technical assistance and letting me use his computer. A special thanks to L T for sharing the Original Survey and Map of Lem Taylor Tract of Land – done by Don. G. Nolte – Licensed State Land Surveyor of Mt. Pleasant, Texas dated June 1946.

Prologue

There were no pictures taken of Lem Taylor while he was alive. According to Marie, Clay and L T looked a lot like him. Lem was a Land Owner and a Farmer. He owned 160 acres of land in the early '20s. Lem's family farmed and lived off the fruits of the land. Lem also owned a Syrup Mill and employed a lot of people to work for him. He owned 2 cars, one of which was a Model "T" Ford. The second car the siblings couldn't remember the type or make of the car. He supplied the Daingerfield High School for Negroes, wood (from the trees on his land) during the winter.

Lem agreed to sell the 160 acres of land to the Federal Government for the Civilian Conservation Corps Camp (CCC Camp). Lem wanted to move his family closer to the Town of Daingerfield, Texas. He then purchased 6.3.10th acres of land from Lawrence B. Jenkins and built a new house in the early

'30s. Lem gave each of his children a plot of land that was equal in area and was 0.549 acres each. There were 11 equal lots, rather than 12, for the number of children Lem and Leah had. Lem's son Hardy was 18 years old when he was killed by a CCC Camp truck driver in 1939. He had no offspring to get his lot of land, and that was the reason for the 11 lots. According to L T, Clay was like his father in regards to his character and family values. They both wanted their children to learn a Trade or go to College. Lem Taylor instilled in his children the importance of family and the value of owning land. Even though Lem did not know his father, he made certain that each of his children knew him and what he stood for. Lem left his "Brand" on each of the Taylor children, and it is reflected in the grandchildren as well as the great, great, great-grandchildren. The Taylor / Lewis Genes are strong and filled with lots of youthfulness, vitality and longevity.

Lem Taylor was also involved in the community. He was President of the P.T.A. from 1927 to 1928. He was a member of the NAACP and a Deacon at the New Hope Baptist Church.

Part I
Narratives of the Early Years

Lem owned 160 acres of land in the early '20s where the Taylor family resided. They farmed and lived off the fruits of the land. The Syrup Mill that Lem owned was also on the land which was located beyond their house. Lem employed a lot of people to work for him at the Syrup Mill. There were two white families and Lem's family that owned land. They were asked to sell their land to the Federal Government for the Civilian Conservation Corps Camp (CCC Camp). According to the Taylor siblings, their father agreed to sell the land. L T reported that Lem wanted to move the family closer to the town of Daingerfield. Lem's 160 acres is the current site of the Daingerfield State Park. In the early '30s, Lem purchased six and three-tenths acres of land from Lawrence B. Jenkins and secured a financial loan from Buster Williams to build a new house (the site where L T lives today). According to L T, Buster Williams' son – Dud Williams the owner of the lumber yard, wanted the land and tried to buy it.

The property is right on State Highway No.49. The Subdivision of the Lem Taylor Tract of Land is just east of the City of Daingerfield, Morris County Texas - Being part of the Allen Urquhart Survey and part of the Isaac T.Bruton Survey. Each of the Eleven Lots in the Subdivision is equal in Area and is 0.549 Acres. The Deed to the Original Tract is filed in Morris County Deed of Records Vol. II Page 152. Lot -1 is assigned to Gatisy Taylor–Edney, Lot- 2 assigned to

Vivian Taylor- Jones, Lot -3 assigned to Igie Taylor- Scott, Lot- 4 assigned to Maggie Taylor- Hatten, Lot- 5 assigned to Marie Taylor, Lot- 6 assigned to Central Taylor, Lot -7 assigned to Corine Taylor-Hill, Lot -8 assigned to L T Taylor, Lot- 9 assigned to Luster Taylor, Lot -10 assigned to Clay Taylor and Lot -11 assigned to Dee Taylor. Vivian bought Lot- 4 from Maggie and Clay bought Lot -11 from Dee. The Survey and Map was done by Don. G. Nolte- Licensed State Land Surveyor of Mt. Pleasant, Texas in June 1946. According to L T, he had the land surveyed 3 months after his mother Leah died in March 1946. The city limit had to be changed in order to get running water and electricity in that area.

Clay built his new house on lot 10. The house was small and during the early 30's and 40's, it was known as a "Shotgun House." You could look straight through from the front door to the back door. As Clay's family grew in size, additional rooms were added onto the house. Clay used lot -11 for his large vegetable garden. The garden consisted of a variety of peas, string beans, butter squash, tomatoes, corn, sweet potato, turnip greens, Irish potato, peppers, onions, cabbage, cucumbers and watermelons. Clay continued the farming tradition. He did a lot of Share -Cropping during the '40s and early '50s. However, he did not allow his wife Lula to work in the field. He had horses/ mules, cows, pigs and chickens. Clay also owned a boat and caught a lot of fish. Clay made sure that his siblings and children were supplied with fresh vegetables and meat. The Taylor land was rich with a large Orchard located right next to the family residence- it consisted of apples, peaches, plums, apricots and pecans.

Lem's children had little or no memory of their grandmother Hannah, whom they called "Aunt Puss." Marie's memory of her grandmother was that she had very long braids that were parted down the middle, and that she looked like an Indian. L T stated that his Papa never talked about his family much and he never knew his biological father. Hannah lived with her daughter Donella also known as "Donnie."- They resided way out in the country and had to walk when they visited the rest of the family. The visits occurred on Saturdays. According to L T, Hannah and Donnie would stay about 2 to 3 hours before returning home.

There were no pictures taken of Lem while he was alive. However, according to Marie, Clay and L T looked a lot like him. Lem also owned 2 Cars- one was a Model "T" Ford and the second one, none of the siblings could remember the type or make of the car. It was reported by Lem's children that he never said a curse word in his life.

Lem was President of the PTA in 1927-1928. Lem also supplied wood to the Daingerfield High School for Negroes (DHS) for the winter until it burned down in 1931. L T's memory of his father was that Lem was mean, but was a good daddy. According to L T, his father was a strong disciplinarian and wanted everything done right. L T stated that he knew his father loved them, but he never showed any outward affection towards any of the kids. L T also reported that his brother Dee left home when he was about 17 or 18 years old because of Lem's discipline methods. Dee did not return home until after Lem died in 1936. L T stated that what Lem valued most was taking care of his family. Lem was a good provider and a good farmer. The family had to wake up around 3 or 4 o'clock every morning to get ready to work in the field by 5:30 a.m. They worked until it was dust dark or until Lem said it was quitting time. Leah worked in the field along with everyone else. According to L T, Lem never played with them. He was more of a business man and a hard worker.

Lem was also a deacon at New Hope Baptist Church and a member of the NAACP. According to L T, his brother Clay was a lot like Lem in regards to his character and family values. They both wanted their children to learn a trade or go to College. Lem instilled in his children the importance of family and the value of owning land. Even though Lem did not know his father, he made certain that each of his children knew him and what he stood for. Lem left his "Brand" on each of the Taylor children. The Taylor/Lewis genes are strong and filled with youthfulness, vitality and longevity.

L T also stated that his mother Leah was the manager of the money and the caretaker of the family. She made sure that Lem's method of discipline was not too harsh. Leah had to also use some form of discipline on the children from time to time. Leah ensured that all of her children's needs were met. They always had plenty of food to eat. Leah was a seamstress and made most of the kids' clothes. However, at Christmas time, the children would order new clothes from Sears Roebuck & Company or Montgomery Wards. Lem's children grew up having a piano and a lot of books in the home and L T could play the piano somewhat by ear. L T reported that after the school burned down in 1931, Lem donated their piano to the school. The DHS school faculty and students raised enough money to buy another piano for Lem.

When Lem Taylor died in 1936, Luster was residing in Jefferson, Texas and working as a chauffeur for a Mr. Webb. Luster's first wife Rosetta Taylor was the maid. L T reported that Luster had his brother, Central Taylor, move to Jefferson to farm some land there. Leah had Luster move back to Daingerfield to take over the farm since he was the oldest son. According to L T, his mother needed Luster to help her in raising the other children. Luster and Rosetta ended up getting a divorce. Luster later got married to Mabel Burns -Taylor of Omaha, Texas.

In 1938, Leah received a financial settlement as a result of her son Hardy's death, which she used to pay off the loan on the house to Buster Williams. Hardy was killed at age 18 by a CCC Camp truck near the Taylor residence. According to the surviving siblings, the truck driver swerved out at Hardy and the back end of the long-bed truck struck him in the head, leaving a large hole. Hardy never regained consciousness and was in a coma until he died. According to L T, they were all walking down the road when the incident occurred in 1938. Hardy was a senior in High School and died before he had a chance to graduate.

Leah had a beautiful China Cabinet/ Hutch that she left for Ira Lee- one of her oldest granddaughters. Ira Lee sold the China Cabinet/Hutch to her aunt Marie. The antique Cabinet/Hutch is still in mint condition and continues to be cherished by Aunt Marie for over 60+ years.

Clay Taylor Sr. was a proud man and very family focused. When Ira Lee was pregnant with Phillip, Clay made sure that the baby was not born out of wedlock. He made Robert Austin also known as "Ped," marry his daughter Ira Lee. In the old days, this was known as a "Shot Gun Wedding." Ira Lee and Ped were married and later divorced. The family utilized the help of a Midwife with each child's birth until the late '50s. Ira Lee and Ped's child, Phillip, was raised by his maternal grandparents, Clay and Lula Taylor.

During the '30s and '40s, before the Taylor's had running water and electricity, they had to dig a well for their water supply. The family burned kerosene oil lamps for light. Outhouses were built, since there were no indoor toilets at that time. For bath water, the Taylor's had to heat the water from the well on a wood burning stove. The family took baths once a week in a large round galvanize tub, and all the children had to use the same bath water. The soap that was used to wash their clothes was made from cooking fat (grease) and lye. In the backyard, the family used a huge cast iron pot and built a fire under it to boil the white clothes. They also used the old fashioned washboard to clean the clothes.

When the family slaughtered a pig or cow, the meat was preserved and stored in a Smokehouse. Salt was used to preserve the meat. The family also did a lot of canning to preserve the abundance of fruit and vegetables that they grew. They had cows that produced a lot of milk, and the family used the old fashion churn to make butter. There were no chemicals used in the feed given to the farm animals and chickens. Therefore, the food was completely organic.

The Taylor family was avid church goers and read the Bible a lot. When you joined the church and were baptized, the Preacher and members of the church would gather at the pond for the ceremony. A deacon would be on both sides of you while you held your nose, the deacons would lean you backwards until your head was completely submerged under water and then lift you back up.

Clay Taylor Sr.'s family always had their dinner together and each member had to say grace before eating. The family celebrated the traditional holidays together.

The Taylor family had a lot of family reunions. There were a lot of great food, games of dominoes and music. The reunions were held in the following locations: Daingerfield, Marshall, Dallas, Hughes Springs, all of which are in Texas, in addition to California and Oklahoma City, OK. The last family reunion was held in Dallas, Texas on July 13, 2002. The next family reunion in planned for the middle on July in 2008, in East Texas.

Part II
Lem Taylor's History

PARENTS:

Mother: **Hannah Taylor** DOB: Unknown – DOD: Unknown

Part Indian / **Taylor** could have been her slave name

(**Lem's** mother / **Clay's** Grandmother / **Mary Taylor's** Paternal Great Grandmother)

Father: Unknown

Lem Taylor: DOB: March 5, 1875 – (known as "**Papa**" by his children) – Land Owner – Owner of Syrup Mill – Provided wood from the trees on his land to the Daingerfield High School for Negroes during the winter – Left handed – When **Lem** was born **Ulysses S. Grant** was the 18th **President** of the **United States** from 1869 – 1877

DOD: May 19, 1936 (Died of Pneumonia at age 61) – When **Lem** died **Franklin D. Roosevelt** was the 32nd **President** of the **United States** from 1933 – 1945 - Married to **Leah Lewis-Taylor** they had 12 Children:

Lem's Siblings:

Lizzie Taylor – DOB: Unknown – DOD: Unknown - no children – deceased

Leonard "Bozie" Taylor – also known as **"Uncle Bud"**- DOB: Unknown – DOD: Unknown – half brother – never married – no children – half white – deceased

Donella Taylor – also known as **"Donnie"** – DOB: Unknown – DOD: Unknown – She had **6 children**:

> **Lillie B. Taylor** – DOB: Unknown – DOD: Unknown – deceased – had 1 child, **Cotille.**

> **O.D. Taylor** – DOB: Unknown – DOD: Unknown – straight hair – no children – half white

> **Sylvester James** – DOB: Unknown – No. of children unknown

> **Ennis James** – DOB: Unknown – No. of children unknown

> **Lettie Mae Taylor** – also known as **"Dude"** – DOB: Unknown – deceased - no children - resided in Dallas, Texas and

> **Damon Taylor** – DOB: Unknown – DOD: Unknown – deceased–- no children

Henry Taylor - DOB: Unknown – DOD: Unknown – deceased – He had **4 Children**:

Ollie Dean Taylor (died at 85 yrs)

Peter Taylor

Fadental Taylor and **George Alley Taylor** (all deceased)

Wade Taylor- DOB: Unknown – DOD: Unknown – half brother – no children – half white – deceased.

Lem and Leah's 12 Children:

Igie Taylor-Scott – DOB: October 23, 1901 – DOD: December 10, 2003 – married to **George Scott** – deceased – resided in Lubbock, Texas. Igie relocated to San Diego, CA to stay with her son **David Walton** – DOB: April 1, 1920 – (87 years old) **David** has been in San Diego since 1940 – married 1ˢᵗ wife **Maudie Lee** they divorced – he then married his 2ⁿᵈ wife Virginia – deceased – **David's** father is **Andor Walton** – deceased – resided in Wills Point, Texas – **David** is a horticulturist (Roses) – raised from infancy by his maternal grandparents (**Lem** and **Leah Taylor**) – His mother Igie died at age 102. (It is important to note that **David** gave **Mary Taylor (Langford)** a gold Bulova watch upon graduating from High School in 1957. To this day, **Mary** still has the watch).

15

Luster Taylor – also known as **"Tut"** – DOB: February 2, 1903 (Ground Hog Day) – DOD: August 9, 1981 – died at age 78 – 1st wife was **Rosetta Taylor** – **Luster** worked in Jefferson, Texas as a Chauffeur in the '30s – divorced and married **Mabel Burns-Taylor** – his 2nd wife – **Mabel's** DOB: September 4, 1912

Mabel's DOD: November 23, 1998 – they had no children.

Central Taylor – also known as **"Nat"** – DOB: November 14, 1905- DOD: May 24, 1975 – died at age 70 – Married to **Louie Mendel Figures-Taylor** – DOB: July 16, 1911 – DOD: August 14, 1995 – died at age 84

They had 6 children:

Doris Ann Taylor-Hardiman – DOB: April 29, 1928 – DOD: April 27, 1986 – died at age 58 – married **Thomas G. Hardiman** – deceased – had a step-son **Richard C. Hardiman** – also deceased – **Richard** was the Band Director at JJ Rhoads High in the early '60s. He was a great Saxophonist and played R&B with local Bands in East Texas. **Richard's** wife **Gloria Hardiman** was the 11th Grade History Teacher at JJ Rhoads High.

Estelle La Verne Taylor-Flemings – DOB: December 21, 1929 – married to **Leo W. Flemings** – they had 2 children: 1 boy and 1 girl – resides in El Paso, Texas.

Harold Taylor- DOB: January 9, 1932 – DOD: March 28, 1990 – died at age 58 – married **Annette Taylor** – had 5 children – resided in California.

Joyce Marie Taylor-Moore – DOB: January 7, 1935 – married **Alexander A. Moore** – no children – Nurse – resides in Lufkin, Texas

Eunice Faye Taylor-Dunda- DOB: December 24, 1936 – married to **S. Kitova Dunda** – no children – resides in Vancouver, WA

Ralph Paul Taylor- resides in Lufkin, Texas – married to **Jackie** – they have 6 children: **Darren Taylor, Brandi Taylor – Grey, Kellee Taylor- Shorts, Ralph P Taylor Jr.** and **Shannon Taylor. Shannon** lives in Lufkin, TX, The other children live in Southern California.

Maggie Taylor-Hatten- also known as **"Sue"** – DOB: January 7, 1907 – DOD: February 24, 1994 – **Maggie** was 87 years old at the time of her death. She completed Cosmetology at Espanola Beauty School in Marshall, Texas. She was married to **James Hatten**, who preceded her in death. They had no children. **Maggie** resided in Daingerfield, Texas at the time of her death.

Clay Taylor Sr. - also known as "**Samp**" – DOB: May 2, 1908 – DOD: September 24, 1994 – His death occurred 2 months after his son **Lem** and **Aunt Emma** died and 7 months after his sister **Maggie** died. **Clay's** death was a result of having leukemic blood cells that turned into the quickly fatal form. He also had glaucoma and cataracts in both eyes and had surgery to correct the problem. Clay's lungs were completely destroyed from working at Long Star Steel Plant. A Class Action Suit was filed against the Plant and a financial settlement was made. He died at age 86. **Clay** married **Lula Bernice Elkins -Taylor** – also known as "**Big Mama**" – on October 28, 1928, at age 19 and **Lula** was 15 years old. **Lula Taylor** died on June 27, 1980 – Clay was a member of the McKinley Masonic Lodge #440 and also a member of the NAACP – Retired at age 50 from Lone Star Steel Plant as a Crane Operator and Foreman after 24 years of service. He also reared 2 grandchildren (**Phillip Austin** and **Gloria Roney**). After 52 years of marriage and **Lula Taylor** died, **Clay** remarried twice. The 2 wives preceded him in death. **Clay Taylor Sr.** had: 32 grandchildren, 54 great-grandchildren, and 4 great-great grandchildren.

Clay and Lula's Children:

<u>Ira Lee Taylor – Austin -Evans</u> – DOB: August 23, 1929 – Retired – resided in Denton, Texas where she and her 2nd husband raised their 6 children – 1st husband was **Robert Austin** – also known as "**Ped**" – **Phillip**'s father. 2nd husband was **James Melvin Evans** – also known as "**Jim**" and the father of the other 6 children – **Ira Lee** and **Jim** got divorced and she moved to Dallas with her children – **Jim** died August 17, 1994.

Ira Lee had 7 children:

(1) **Phillip Austin** DOB: January 17, 1947 – married to **Salome Bates-Austin** – they had 2 children:

Kevin Austin – DOB: June 2, 1971- graduated from North Texas State with a Degree in Accounting-works for Verizon in Dallas, Texas. **Kedrick Austin** – DOB: December, 25, 1977 – Graduated from North Texas State with a Degree in Accounting-works for Chase Bank as a Financial Loan Officer. **Phillip** – attended Cedar Valley Community College and Mountain View Community College toward an Engineering Degree- employed at the U.S. Post Office in Dallas, Texas for 31 years-plan to retire in 2008 – **Phillip's** wife **Salome** is Supervisor of Probation with the State Parole.

(2) **Gwendolyn Evans – James** DOB: October 2, 1950 – Married **Robert James Jr. – Robert** is deceased – They had **4 children:**

Warren Evans, Policeman in Wichita, KS-divorced and has 2 children: **Jorda Renee Evans** and **Trevon Evans**

April James-Aimes – DOB: March 12, 1972, divorced and has 2 children **Derrick Aimes** and **Jacoby Aimes- April** works as a Financial Officer in Dallas;

Kendal James – Manager at Coca-Cola Company in Wichita, KS

Robert James, III – a Muslim, known as **Prince Ali-** resides in San Antonio, TX – also studying International Law

(3) **Marilyn Evans-Dixon** – DOB: November 7, 1955 – divorced and has 3 girls:

Latoya (Toy) Jones DOB: March 1, 1974 – teacher in Terrell, TX – Married – has 2 children: **Aisja Te`lor Jones** and **Wynter Noelle Jones**.

Devon (Dev) Evans – DOB: May 12, 1983 – Graduated from the University of Texas at Austin on May 18, 2007 – 1ˢᵗ Year Teacher in Terrell, Texas

DiAnte Evans (Pooh) DOB: August 13, 1980 – has 4 children: **Brooklyn Evans, Kynedie McCallister, Trinity Leah Evans** and **Daillon James McCallister**.

(4) Sandra Evans – Boggs – also known as "**Candi**" – DOB: March 14, 1959 – married to **Ralph Boggs** an Engineer at Texas Instrument on March 15, 2007 – no children – **Candi** retired from Texas Instrument at age 48

(5) Anthony Evans – DOB: March 5, 1952 – Licensed Plumber – served in the U.S. Marine – married **Linda Young-Evans** – divorced and had 4 children: **Nicole** age 12 the youngest, mother is white. **Nicole** resides with her paternal grandmother, **Ira Lee; Christie Evans-Patton** age 33, resides in Denton, Texas; **Andrea Leah Evans** age 35, has 3 children: 2-boys and 1-girl and **Anthony Evans Jr.** age 34

(6) James Melvin Evans, III – also known as **"Peewee"** – DOB: October 13, 1957 – has 1 child – Served in the U. S. Marine – Licensed Plumber and Long Haul Tractor – Trailer Driver and

(7) Elaine Evans – DOB: October 28, 1954 – DOD: March 30, 1956 – died at 17 months old.

Clay Taylor Jr. – also known as **"Jack"** – DOB: May 20, 1931 – DOD: July 16, 2002, of a heart attack at age 71 – married to **Bessie Quarnell Connally** on July 7, 1957 – served in the United States Army from October 28, 1952 to June 9, 1954. He was ranked as Corporal – received the "Medal of Honor" for good conduct, upon his honorable discharge. Attended Wiley College for 3 years and resided in Dallas, TX. Deacon at the Star of Bethlehem Baptist Church and was awarded: "Man of the Year" plaque in 1996 and a "Tribute of Love and Appreciation" plaque in 1999. Clay Jr. was a gifted speaker and teacher of the "Word" of God. They had **5 children:**

(1) Patricia Taylor – has 3 children: **Dachsha Taylor**- he has 3 children: **Dachsha Taylor Jr.** (7), **Kameron Denise Taylor** (4) and **Iman (Nay Nay) Taylor** (5); **Patricia's** fraternal twins-boy – **Cashmen Taylor Jones** DOB: July 6, 1991 and girl – **Cashton Taylor Jones**

DOB: July 7, 1991 – **Patricia** works for FEDEx and resides in Fort Worth, Texas.

(2) Dennis Earl Taylor DOB: March 22, 1960-DOD: June 29, 2001 – died from a heart attack at age 41 – married **Eleanor.** They had 6 children; **Dennis Taylor Jr., Deangelo Taylor, Dylan Taylor, Tegria Taylor, Rita Taylor** and **Jamaica Reed.**

(3) Tina Taylor (deceased 2003) and

(4) Toni Taylor (Twins) **Toni** has 1 child: **Milik Sullemon** age 12 – **Toni** is employed by Home Land Security, at Love Field Airport in Dallas, Texas and

(5) Gregory Scott Taylor DOB: July 29, 1966 – DOD: June 23, 2007 – died at age 41 – had 1 child-**Shamekia Taylor. Bessie Taylor** resides in Dallas, TX – **Clay Taylor Jr.** is buried at Dallas-Fort Worth National Cemetery in Dallas, Texas.

<u>Imogene Taylor-Roney</u> – DOB: July 4, 1932 (deceased) died of breast cancer in 1976 at age 44. Married **Joe Melvin Roney** and resided in Dallas TX. Short – Order Cook. They had **6 children:**

Gloria Roney DOB: May 27, 1958 – Nurse – (2 sons: **Terrence Turner** and **Joshua Mitchell** – they reside in Daingerfield, Texas.

Charles Roney

James Roney

Joe Melvin Roney Jr.

Billy Roney and

Glen Roney

<u>**Josephine Taylor-Parker**</u> – DOB: January 8, 1934 – DOD: January 25, 1983 – died at age 49 – Ran away from home in the early '50s, resurfaced 5 years later, and had gotten married. She was residing at that time in Wichita Falls, Texas. She later divorced and relocated to Dallas, Texas. She was killed while employed at the Dallas Morning News and the Dallas Times Herald. The murder suspect was never found. She had no children.

<u>**Lem Taylor**</u> – DOB: November 10, 1936 – DOD: July 11, 1994 – Died from heart attack at age 58. In the early '50s, he was incarcerated in the Huntsville, Texas jail for stealing. **Lem's** 1st wife was **Mae Otis Taylor** – they had 2 sons - divorced – He

later married **Georgia Crump – Taylor** in 1989- **Lem** had 1 daughter and 8 sons:

Sharon Taylor – reside in Aurora, NC

Lemuel Taylor reside in Daingerfield, Texas

Gary Taylor resides in Daingerfield, Texas

Kevin Taylor of Mt. Pleasant, Texas

Kent Taylor of New Orleans, LA

Brent Taylor of New Orleans, LA

Charles Crump of Alexandria, VA

Willie Williams of Alexandria, VA

Terry Williams of Aurora, NC.

Lem relocated to North Carolina in 1980 as General Foreman with Brown & Root Construction CO out of Shreveport, Louisiana.

Mary L. Taylor-Langford – also known as **"Mema"** DOB: October 2, 1938 – born in Harrison County, Marshall, Texas. Married to **Harold F. Langford, Jr.,** July 7, 1961, in Marshall,

TX. She was awarded a 4 year scholarship in Music to Bishop College in August 1957. **Mary** graduated from Bishop College in 1961 with a Bachelor of Science Degree in Music with Emphasis on Voice. She was also awarded a 4 year scholarship in Music to the University of Indiana Graduate School in 1961 and was 3rd place winner of a **"Bathing Suit Beauty Contest"** with **Dick Clark** America Bandstand in 1966. She moved from Texarkana, TX in 1972, and relocated to Springfield, Massachusetts. She received a Masters Degree in Psychology from the University of Massachusetts at Amherst, MA in 1978. She is the author of "**Mister Buddha**" written in September 2002. **Mary** retired from The Commonwealth of Massachusetts Department of Social Services on May 30, 2005 as Manager of the Foster Care, Adoption and Permanency Planning Units. She had Total Hip Replacement on May 17, 2007 after being diagnosed with having congenital dislocation of the right hip. She has since fully recovered. They had **4 Children**:

(1) Harold F. Langford, III, the oldest also known as **"Lil' Harold,"** and **"Gus"**- DOB: June 3, 1962 – born in Morris County, Daingerfield, Texas – Retired Correctional Officer at Hampden County Correctional Facility in Ludlow, MA, **Harold, III** has 3 children: oldest daughter adopted at birth, 2nd oldest – **Sommerlyn Mckenzie Taylor-Langford** DOB: May 23, 1999, also known as "**Little Miss Pookie Head**", her father calls her **"Pumpkin"** and the youngest – **Chase Harrison**

Langford DOB: July 29, 2002 – blond hair, blue eyed, his father calls him **"Little Man", Sommer** and **Chase's** mother is **Brenda Jones**

(2) Robin Michelle Langford, the second oldest Born: June 15, 1963 at Parkland Memorial Hospital in Dallas, Texas – It is important to note that Parkland Memorial Hospital is where **President John F. Kennedy** died after being assassinated in Dallas, Texas in 1963 – **Robin Michelle** died on November 23, 1963 of Hydrocephalus in Texarkana, Texas – 5 months old at time of death.

(3) Charles T. Langford – the third oldest also known as **"Chuck,"** DOB: May 11, 1969 – born in Texarkana, Texas – a Jazz Musician –Attended the University of Massachusetts at Amherst and the New School of Jazz And Contemporary Music in New York, N.Y. – Has played in most of the major cities in the U.S., Canada, and Europe. Teaches private Saxophone lessons to 25 to 30 students (weekly) – Has a Web Site (myspace) and currently working on the final touches of a CD – Married **Catherine Estrela-Langford** –on November 11, 2006, has a step-daughter **Lizzie Estrela** DOB: August 4, 1997; and

(4) Virna L. Campbell-Langford – the youngest-also known as **"Ms V"** and **"Auntie VeeVee"** – DOB:

February 16, 1971- born in Texarkana, Texas – a fifth grade teacher and Recording Engineer – Has a Recording Studio- Bachelor Degree in Psychology from The University of Massachusetts at Amherst, MA-Currently enrolled at Elm's College working towards her Masters Degree – married to **Michele Campbell** on July 12, 2002, Assistant Principal in Springfield Public School System.

Robert Taylor – DOB: June 3, 1947 – Attended Bishop College for 3 years and East Texas State for 1 year – Served in the U.S. Army – married **Evelyn Minter-Taylor** on November 9, 1969/ had one child: **Rosalind Taylor. Robert** remarried to **Alexis Taylor** (no children from this marriage) – resides in Irving, Texas – Retired from Sears- currently employed – Plays Piano and Organ for his Church- **Alexis Taylor** is a Preacher.

Margaret Ann Taylor – DOB: October 22, 1948 – DOD: April 14, 1959 (died from Leukemia at age 10)

Corine Taylor-Hill – DOB: March 6, 1910 – DOD: June 19, 1939 at age 29 – While the family was planning to celebrate the Juneteenth (Black Texans were freed on the 19th of June 1865 by General Sheriden), **Marie** went to get **Corine** and found her dead. **Corine** was married to **Charlie Hill**.

They had 2 sons: **Charles** and **Clarence Hill** –**Clarence** also known as **"Squeaky."** After **Corine's** death, **Charlie Hill** and the 2 boys relocated to Los Angeles, CA. **Charlie** later remarried.

Dee Taylor – DOB: February 9, 1912 – DOD: November 14, 1978 at age 66 – left home at an early age around 17 or 18 due to his father's discipline methods. He didn't return home until after his father died in 1936. **Dee** had also gotten married to a woman named **Alice**, she had 2 girls and a boy – **Dee** was an Auto Mechanic – owned an Auto Shop in Mt Pleasant, Texas- he also owned an Auto Body Shop in Los Angeles. He resided in Los Angeles, CA at the time of his death – married twice – no children.

Marie Taylor – also known as **"Babe"** – DOB: February 11, 1914 – (93 years old) and still going strong – married to **Lee O. Taylor** (deceased) DOD: Aug 17, 2000. **Marie** was a Licensed Beautician – owned a Beauty Solon. She graduated from Bishop College in the early '40s. **Marie** is a retired Special Education Teacher from the Marshall Public School System. She resides in Marshall, Texas. **Marie** had 1 child: **Alfred Ray Taylor** (adopted at birth). **Alfred's** first wife was **Marilyn Trammel-Taylor** they had 1-daughter: **Angela Taylor** (27) resides in Dallas Texas – **Alfred** resides in Longview, Texas with second wife and son **Aaron Taylor** (10) – **Marie Taylor** is diabetic and on insulin-had laser surgery on both eyes – total knee replacement on both knees and a total hip replacement.

Gatisy Taylor-Edney – also known as **"Kitty"** – DOB: June 21, 1916 – (91 years old) resides in Oklahoma City, OK – married **Dorothy Edney** – deceased – **Gatisy** and **Dorothy** moved to Oklahoma City, OK in 1937 – they had 2 daughters:

> **Gloria Dickerson** – DOB: December 8, 1931-DOD: January 10, 1987 – died at age 56 – married to **Jimmy Dickerson** – **Gloria** was employed at the Skirvin Hotel in Oklahoma City for 31 years – had 3 children:

> **Gregg Simpson** – deceased 4 or 5 years ago – has 1 son: **Gregg Simpson Jr.** reside in Oklahoma City, OK

> **Timothy Smith** is in Helena, Oklahoma Prison – Received life Sentence for killing his mother **Gloria** in January 1987 due to drug involvement – has 1 son: **Jermaine Smith** – reside in Oklahoma City, OK

> **Kim Atchison** – married to **Lawrence Atchison** of Albuquerque, NM – has 2 adopted children: **Steven Atchison** (18), starting College in Abilene, Texas fall of 2007 and **Melody Atchison** (13)

Oreatha Edney- Sheets – DOB: March 24, 1936 – reside in Tulsa, Ok –Divorced – They have **3 children**:

Joe Ray Sheets Jr.

Michael Hill and

Theresa Diana Sheets-Foster – **Theresa** has 2 children: **Anthony Washington** and **Angela Washington** – **Anthony** has 2 children: **Creighton Washington** (6), **Corbin Washington** (4) and **Angela** (26) – single – no children – on active duty in the Navy – will be attending graduate school in Florida – fall of 2007; **Oreatha Sheets** is a cancer survivor (rectal).

LT Taylor – DOB: Aug 21, 1918 – (89 years old) – also known as "**Skinner**" – married to **Lucille Hickman-Taylor** (**Lula Elkins'** half sister) Date of Marriage: August 20, 1940 – **Lucille** graduated from high school in Naples, Texas in 1933. She was accepted at Bishop College and attended for one day when her father **Rob Hickman** died. **Lucille** had to leave school to take care of her mother **Fannie Lou.** She never returned to Bishop College. – **Lucille Hickman-Taylor** died on April 11, 1998 – no children – **L T Taylor** is diabetic and on insulin – Retired from Lone Star Steel Plant – Reside in Daingerfield, Texas.

Hardy Taylor – DOB: March 16, 1920 – DOD: April 1, 1938 – killed at age 18 by a CCC Camp truck near the Taylor residence – According to the surviving siblings, the driver of the CCC Camp truck, swerved out at **Hardy** and the back end of the long-bed truck, struck **Hardy** in the head- leaving a large hole. **Hardy** never regained consciousness and was in a coma until he died. **Hardy's** siblings witnessed the accident – **L T** reported that they were all walking down the road when the incident occurred in the late '30s. The family went to court and a financial settlement was made. **Hardy** was a High School senior at the time of his death and died before he had a chance to graduate.

Vivian Lavon Taylor-Jones – also known as **"Patty"** – DOB July 1, 1922 – (85 years old) – Left home at age 18 – stayed with her cousin **Freddie Mack** in Kansas City, Missouri for a while – she then relocated to Oklahoma City, OK to stay with her sister **Kitty** – married to **Herman Jones** (deceased) of Oklahoma City. **Patty** is a Licensed Beautician – Owner of Beauty Shop- still working with a few selected clienteles. When **Patty** was 2 years old, she imitated her sister **Kitty** by sitting on the churn. She fell into the churn and couldn't get out. **Patty's** head and legs were the only things visible and her mother **Leah** had to break the churn to get her out. They had 2 daughters:

Patricia Jones – DOB: July 18, 1950 – DOD: January 7, 2004 – died at age 54 – no children – (was a teacher); and

Sharian Lavon Jones-Mason-Collins – also known as **"Sister"** – DOB: March 14, 1953 – married twice – divorced – has 3 children: **Rhoderick Mason Jr.** (30)**, Demetria Mason** (27) – has 4 children: **DeAushnia Mason, Joshua Mason, Dejua Mason** and **Teleah Mason;** and **James Collins** (25) – **Sharian** previously worked as an Independent Travel Consultant in Oklahoma City, OK

Part III
Leah Lewis-Taylor's History

Parents:

Mother: **Margaret Lewis** DOB: Unknown – DOD: Unknown

Father: **Peter Lewis** DOB: Unknown – DOD: Unknown

Leah Lewis-Taylor – DOB: January 2, 1878 – (known as **"Mama"** by her children) – DOD: March 13, 1946 – (due to heart problem / enlarged heart and suffered from asthma) – seamstress – a great cook – money manager-and caretaker – When **Leah** was born **Rutherford B. Hayes** was 19th **President** of the **United States** from 1877 – 1881 When **Leah** died **Harry S. Truman** was the 33rd **President** of **the United States** from 1945 – 1953 – **Leah** died at age 68 – Married to **Lem Taylor**

Leah's Siblings:

Clay Lewis – deceased – DOB: unknown – DOD: unknown – No. of children unknown – resided in Gilmer, Texas

Emma Lewis-Reid-Cameron-Howell – DOB: October 18, 1885 in Daingerfield, Texas – DOD: July 12, 1994 – she was 108.9 years old when she died – **Emma** married her 1st husband **Evert Reid** on December 13, 1904 – they had 3 children. She married 2nd husband **Charlie Cameron** in 1917 – they had 1 child. At the age of 12, **Emma** became a member of the Church and worked faithfully until she was 100 years old. During that time, her health began to fail. She served as Superintendent of Sunday School, President of Y.W.A. Council, President of Deacons wives, Treasurer of Sunday School, and Teacher of boys and girls classes. **Emma** served her community as President of the P.T.A., Supervisor of the Canning Program and as a Trained Midwife. She delivered over 75 babies. **Emma** moved to Hammond, LA to live with her daughter **Mable** in 1986. **Emma** has 14 grandchildren, 36 great grandchildren and 2 great, great, great-grandchildren

Emma's 4 Children:

(1) **Ernest Reid** – also known as "**Sport**" – deceased – he has 3 children: **Charles Reid**, **Verma Reid**, and **Ernest Reid Jr.** – also known as "**Buddy**":

(2) **Mable Reid-Nelson** – of Hammond, LA

(3) **Bobbie Reid-Marshall** of Snyder, Texas and

(4) **Meredith Cameron** (deceased)

Anne Bell Lewis-Gilstrap McNealy – DOB: Unknown – DOD: Unknown – died in her '80s – had a hearing problem / Married **Don McNealy**– deceased – (no Children) **Anne Bell** could crochet and knit – had her sister **Earlie** move from Shreveport, Louisiana to Daingerfield, Texas to live with her

– **Anne Bell** was a resident at Windsor Place Nursing home at the time of her death.

Earlie Lewis-Finley Jordan – DOB: Unknown – DOD: Unknown – died in her 70s – the youngest of the siblings – very beautiful lady – gray hair with just a hint of blue) 1ˢᵗ husband was **George Finley** – no children – 2ⁿᵈ husband was **Johnny Jordan** – lived in Shreveport, Louisiana – no children – **Earlie** was a seamstress and worked at a cleaners- heavy smoker – suffered from shortness of breath. **Earlie** moved back to Daingerfield, Texas to live with her sister **Anne Bell. Earlie** died 2 weeks later.

Ola Lewis – DOB: Unknown – DOD: Unknown – had one son: Jodie Gilstrap – married Pearlie Mae, she was diabetic and both legs were amputated – they had 8 children:

(1) **Jodie Clifford Jr.** (deceased)

(2) **Ivory Mae Gilstrap** (deceased)

(3) **Raymond Gilstrap** reside outside of Dallas, TX- graduated from Wiley College – a "Math Genius" – married and has a son

(4) **James Gilstrap** also known as "**Jim**" – (musician) in Los Angeles, CA – Background Singer for a lot of the

Top Major Artists – **Jim** has a daughter who reside in Buffalo, NY

(5) Mabel Gilstrap-Rankins – 69 years old – graduated from Wiley College in Marshall TX – Married **William Rankins** (79) – resided in Dorchester, Massachusetts before relocating to Greensboro, NC in 1972 – has 5 girls: **Claudelle Rankins-Duncan** – The oldest – married to **Terry Duncan**, they have 2 boys: **T. J. Duncan** and **Nicholas Duncan** – served in the U.S Army -resides in Greensboro, NC; **Cynthia Rankins** – 2nd oldest resides in Raleigh, NC; **Cora Rankins** – DOB :February 5, 1965 – 3rd child-resides at home with her father in Greensboro, NC; **Cia Rankins-Kahn** – 4th child – graduated from A&T College with a Degree in English – resides in Greensboro, NC- has no children; and **Chrystal Rankins** – the youngest child-single – and has 1 child: **Maya McCullough** age 8 – resides in Greensboro, NC – served in the U.S. Army. **Mabel** is currently in a Nursing Home in Greensboro, NC – She is diabetic, blind and has Alzheimer's.

(6) Mattie Lee Gilstrap – retired teacher in Los Angeles, CA)

(7) Ola Gilstrap – deceased – resided in Los Angeles, CA; and

(8) George Emery Gilstrap – deceased – was a self made child preacher.

Georgie Lewis – **(deceased)** – had 7 children: live in Daingerfield, TX

Ben Leftwich, Noble Leftwich (teacher/principal), **Willie Leftwich, Clarence Leftwich, Ruthie Leftwich, Pinky Leftwich,** and **Anne Mae Leftwich**

Charlie Lewis – (deceased) had 3 children: **Lurie Lewis, Erman Lewis** and **Arnie Lee Lewis** – had one daughter who taught at JJ Rhoads High: name unknown

Peter Lewis Jr. also known as "**Uncle Pete**" – DOB: Unknown – DOD: Unknown –deceased –

Had **4 children:**

Arlene Lewis – Corporal also known as "**Precious**" – DOB: Unknown

Reyford Lewis DOB: Unknown

Marguerite Estell Lewis – DOB: Unknown – reside in Muncie, KS, and

Freddie Mack Lewis DOB: November 14, 1918 – DOD: June 2, 1988 – died at age 70 – lived in Kansas City for over 50 years- attended and finished the K. C. School of Watch-Making – U.S. Army veteran of World War II, serving in the European Theatre and the South Pacific – was honorably discharged in 1946 – employed by General Motors before retiring after 30 years of service – Buried at Leavenworth National Cemetery in Leavenworth, Kansas. He married **Alma A Miller** on January 7, 1939. **Freddie Mack** had 2 children: **Fredrick W. Lewis** of Atlanta GA and **Clara Evangeline Reese** of Kansas City, MI.

Abby Lewis – DOB: unknown – DOD: unknown – children unknown – in prison for murder – died while incarcerated

Goober Lewis – DOB: unknown – DOD: unknown – children unknown

Cicero Lewis- DOD: December 19, 1880 – DOD: May 19, 1988 – (also known as "**Uncle Cicero**" was 108 years old when he died – resided in Gilmer, Texas – **Cicero's children:**

Nola Hargest of Gilmer, Texas

Augusta Lewis of Fort Worth, Texas

The other children of **Cicero Lewis**, their names are unknown – **Uncle Cicero** has 45 grandchildren, 40 Great-Grandchildren and 60 Great-Great Grandchildren.

Ben Lewis – DOB: unknown – DOD: unknown – has 4 children:

(1) Bee Lewis DOB: unknown – # of children unknown

(2) Ethel Lewis DOB: unknown – No. of children unknown

(3) Jo Dale Lewis-Holloman – DOB: Unknown – of New Jerusalem, Texas – near Daingerfield State Park – married to **John Dee Holloman** on December 6, 1940 – had 2 children: **Dorothy Jean Holloman-Jackson** of Daingerfield, TX and **Jo Dee Holloman** – died October 29, 1966) – he served in the U.S. Air Force – **Jo Dale** is a Quilt and Doll maker – has been quilting since her childhood. She had previously quilted on a home-made frame, but not the old fashioned quilting-bee type that hangs from the ceiling. She is now using the new factory made frame – **Jo Dale** is multi-talented – built a Dress Shop onto her house, when she was in the dress-making business. Some of her dolls are in Germany, Tennessee, California, and San Antonio, TX with nephews and nieces. (This information was taken from an article by **Deborah Sanders** on Wednesday May 11, 1988, title: **"Holloman is Infected with the Relaxing Fever of Quilting"** and

(4) Lonnie Lewis – married to **Viola Lewis** – they had **3 children:**

Ben Allen Lewis – handicap / cerebral palsy, **Cleofas Lewis** and **Dianne Lewis.**

The Taylor/Lewis family possessed a lot of other skills for example: Beautician, Beauty Shop Owners, Seamstresses, Barber, Auto Mechanic, Teachers, Nurses, Trained Midwife, Administrators, Supervisors, Managers, Foreman, Homemakers, Food Preservation Specialists (Fruit/Meat) – known as Canning, Jazz Musicians, Classical/Spiritual Singer, R & B Singer, Recording Engineer, Bathing Suit Beauty – (**Mary T**), Law Student (International Law) – (**Prince Ali**), Writer, an Independent Travel Consultant, A Long Haul Truck Driver, Licensed Plumbers, Licensed Social Worker, Quilt Maker, Doll Maker, Gardener, Fishman and a Karate (Black Belt) – **Harold, III,** Correctional Officer, Water Safety Instructor, Personal Banker, Home Land Security Personnel, Watch-Maker, Dress Shop owner, Beauty Salon Owners, Horticulturist, Accountants, and

Certified Guidance Counselor with the Massachusetts Board of Education.

Military Service: Clay Taylor Jr. – (Army), James Phillip Austin – (Navy), Robert Taylor – (Army), James Melvin Evans, III, – (Marine), Harold F. Langford, III – (Army), Anthony Evans – (Marine) Jo Dee Holloman (Air Force) and Freddie Mack Lewis (World War II Army Vet) Chrystal Gilstrap Rankins (Army), Claudelle Gilstrap Rankins-Duncan (Army) and Angela Sheets Washington (Navy active duty)

Part IV
Hickman / Elkins' History

Parents:

Josephine Flemmings – DOB: Unknown – DOD: Unknown

Lee Flemmings – DOB: Unknown – DOD: Unknown

Fannie Lou Flemmings-Hickman – DOB: March 19, 1898 – DOD: December 13, 1995 – died at age 97 – married **Robert "Rob" Hickman** (**Lucille's** father) – (**Lula's** father's name unknown) – **Lucille** and **Lula** were half-sisters.

Step-mother to **Helen Hickman-Hodge** – **Fannie Lou** was a Quilt maker and a member of the Quilting Bee with her sisters – she was a resident at Windsor Place Nursing Home, at the time of her death – She was diabetic and on insulin – both legs were amputated.

Fannie Lou's Siblings:

Lela Smith – DOB: Unknown – DOD: Unknown – (deceased) – quilt maker – had 2 children:

> **Charlie Roney Sr.** DOB: unknown – DOD: Unknown – Married to **Vivian Deloris Peoples-Roney** – she was born May 14, 1922, and died August 21, 1993 – **Charlie** and **Deloris** were married on October 26, 1940 – he

preceded her in death after 50 years of marriage – they had 9 children:

(1) Charlie Ann Roney-Ray – reside in Dallas, Texas

(2) Gerraine Roney-Benson – reside in Dallas, Texas

(3) Jonette Roney- Bryant – (mother of **Tori** and **Rosalind**) reside in Southlake, Texas

(4) Debbie Roney-Montgomery – reside Pittsburg, Texas

(5) Lisa Roney-Hailey – reside in Desoto, Texas

(6) Alvin Roney – reside in Dallas, Texas

(7) Charlie Roney Jr. – reside in Dallas, Texas

(8) Barry Roney – reside in Pittsburg, Texas

(9) Son that is deceased.

Charlie Roney Sr. a Preacher – has 20 grandchildren, and 16 great-grandchildren resided in Pittsburg, Texas and

Oscar Roney – DOB: Unknown – DOD: Unknown – No. of children unknown

Manerva Woods – DOB: Unknown – DOD: Unknown – quilt maker and member of the Quilting Bee – had **3 children:**

> **Berlin Woods** – DOB: Unknown – Graduated from Joseph J. Rhoads High School in 1948

> **Ernest Woods** – DOB: Unknown – and

> **James Woods** – DOB: Unknown

Lena Bell Fomby – DOB: Unknown – DOD: Unknown – quilt maker and member of the Quilting Bee – (deceased) Not known if she had any children.

Dora Harper – DOB: Unknown – DOD: Unknown – Quilt maker and member of the Quilting Bee – (deceased) – Not known if she had any children.

Fannie Lou's Children:

Lula Bernice Elkins – also known as **"Big Mama"** – DOB: December 2, 1912- DOD: June 27, 1980 – high-blood pressure and was border-line diabetic, also had a stroke – She was 68 years old when she died. (See **Clay Taylor Sr.**) – Dress maker and a hair dresser-

Lucille Fayrene Hickman – DOB: September 6, 1915-DOD: April 11, 1998 (diabetic – was on insulin – both legs amputated – also had a stroke and was unable to speak) **Lucille** was a resident at the Windsor Place Nursing Home in Daingerfield at the time of her death. She was 83 years old. (See **LT Taylor**)

Helen Hickman-Hodge – DOB: Unknown – DOD: Unknown – **Fannie Lou's** step daughter, **Lula's** step-sister, and **Lucille's** half-sister – married to **Hozie Hodge** – they had 3 children: **Steven, Larry,** and **Hozie, Jr.** reside in Oklahoma City, OK – **Helen Hodge** was the daughter of **Rob Hickman** and **Shug** (last name unknown).

Part V
The Taylor Brand

The Taylor / Lewis Family History captures the early '20s and '30s when Lem Taylor owned the 160 acres of land, and agreeing to sell it to the Federal Government for the CCC Camp. It also focuses on the family values, expectation, the purchase of new land and dividing it equally among each child. The History stresses the family constellations and make-up. It also reflects Parenting techniques. It shows vivid pictures of how life was in the old days ('20s, '30s and '40s) — Lem's role in the Church and his involvement in the community. It identified health / medical issues in the family. The Taylor / Lewis family history also focuses on the tragedies within the family, and the reunions that kept them connected.

A Salute to all the surviving siblings: Marie Taylor, Gatisy Taylor-Edney, L T Taylor and Vivian Lavon Taylor-Jones. "May God Continue To Bless Each and Every One of You."

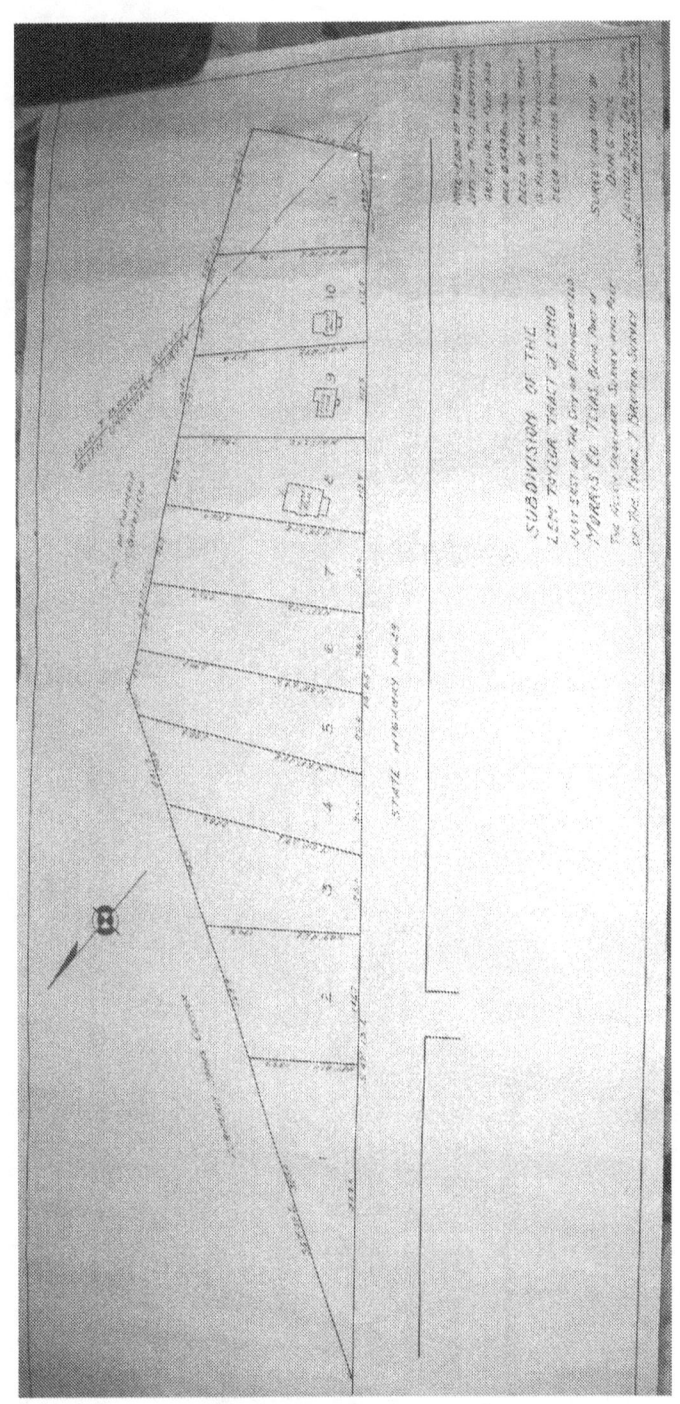

Lem Taylor Tract of Land

Part VI
Pictures

Group picture of the Taylor siblings taken in the '80s

Group picture with children, grandchildren and great-grandchildren taken in the '80s

Patty, Igie, Jo Dale, Kitty and David taken in the late '80s

Family Reunion in Hughes Springs, Texas —
Clay, Gatisy and Igie in the late '80s

Maggie and friend at Family Reunion in Hughes Springs, Texas in the late '80s

Clay's House taken in 1990

Vivian Taylor-Jones and Family December 1992

Luster's House taken in 1990

Marie's 2 Houses taken in 1990

Clay Taylor dressed for Church taken in 1990

L T's House taken in 1990

Clay working in his garden in 1992

Mary Langford

Clay working in his garden 1992

68

Clay in his garden 1992

The Morris Delight Chapter No. 304 of the Eastern Stars – Mary Taylor a member and McKinley Masonic Lodge No. 440 – Clay Taylor Sr. a member taken in 1956

Clay Taylor October 12, 1992

Antique Hutch that belonged to Leah Taylor picture taken in 1990

Lula Bernice Taylor picture taken in the late '60s

Marie Taylor and her husband Lee Overture Taylor
pictures taken in the '60s

Igie Scott at Family Reunion in Hughes Springs,
Texas in the late '80s

L T Taylor and his wife Lucille Taylor picture taken in the '80s

Fannie Lou Hickman picture taken in the '50s

*Gatisy Edney and her sister Maggie Hatten
pictures taken in the late '80s*

*Alexis, Clay, Robert, Langford, Terrence, Mary and Gloria
picture taken October 8, 1993*

Clay and Lula Taylor taken May 12, 1977

*David Walton taken in the late '80s at Family Reunion
in Hughes Springs, Texas*

Clay and Lula Taylor taken May 1964

Family Reunion in Daingerfield, Texas in 1971 –
Imogene Taylor-Roney the one standing

*Clay and Mary Taylor at Family Reunion in
Daingerfield, Texas in 1971*

Family Reunion in Daingerfield, TX in 1971 with Luster Taylor

Dorothy Edney, George Scott and Clay Taylor at
Family reunion in Daingerfield, Texas 1971

Group picture at Family Reunion in
Oklahoma City, OK in the '60s

*April James at Family Reunion on July 4, 1988
in Daingerfield, Texas*

*Mary, Clay, Virna, Fannie Lou and Ira Lee at
Family Reunion July 1988*

*Ralph, Candi, Peewee, Gwen, Ira Lee, Salome, Marilyn and
Phillip at Family Reunion in Dallas, Texas July 13, 2002*

*Mary, Harold, III, Sommer and Chuck at Family reunion in
Dallas July 13, 2002*

Mary and L T at Family Reunion in Dallas July 13, 2002

*Oreatha, Vivian, L T, Gatisy and friends at Family Reunion in
Dallas July 2002*

*More Family Reunion pictures taken in
Dallas, Texas July 13, 2002*

*L T, Vivian, Jack, Ira Lee, Mary and Gatisy at Family Reunion in
Dallas, Texas July 13, 2002*

Ira Lee, Jack and Mary at family reunion in Dallas July 13, 2002

Jack, Scott, Dachsha and friend at family reunion in
Dallas July 13, 2002

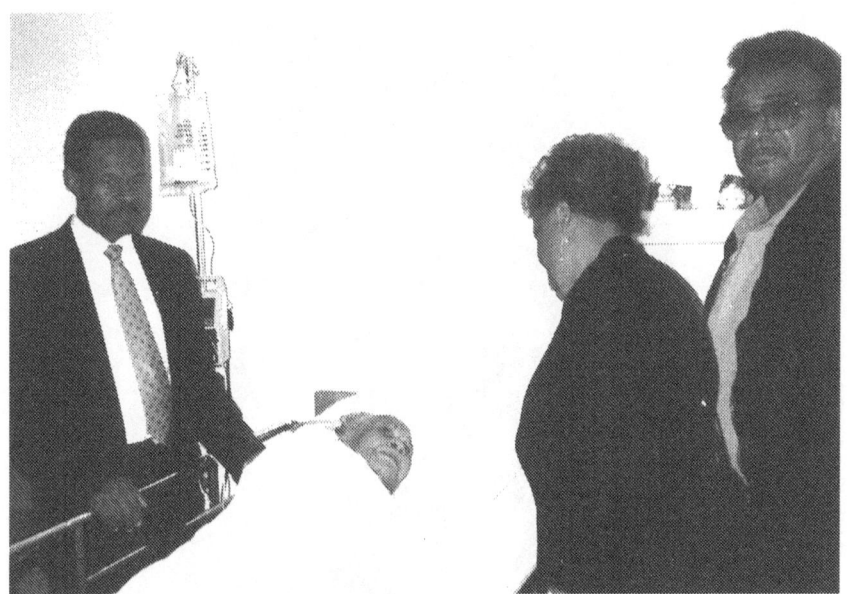

Robert, Fannie Lou, Mary and Langford at Windsor Place
Nursing Home October 1993

Mary, Langford, Clay, Mabel, Alexis and Robert Oct. 1993

Herman and Mary at family reunion in Dallas July 1979

Josephine and Clay December 1979

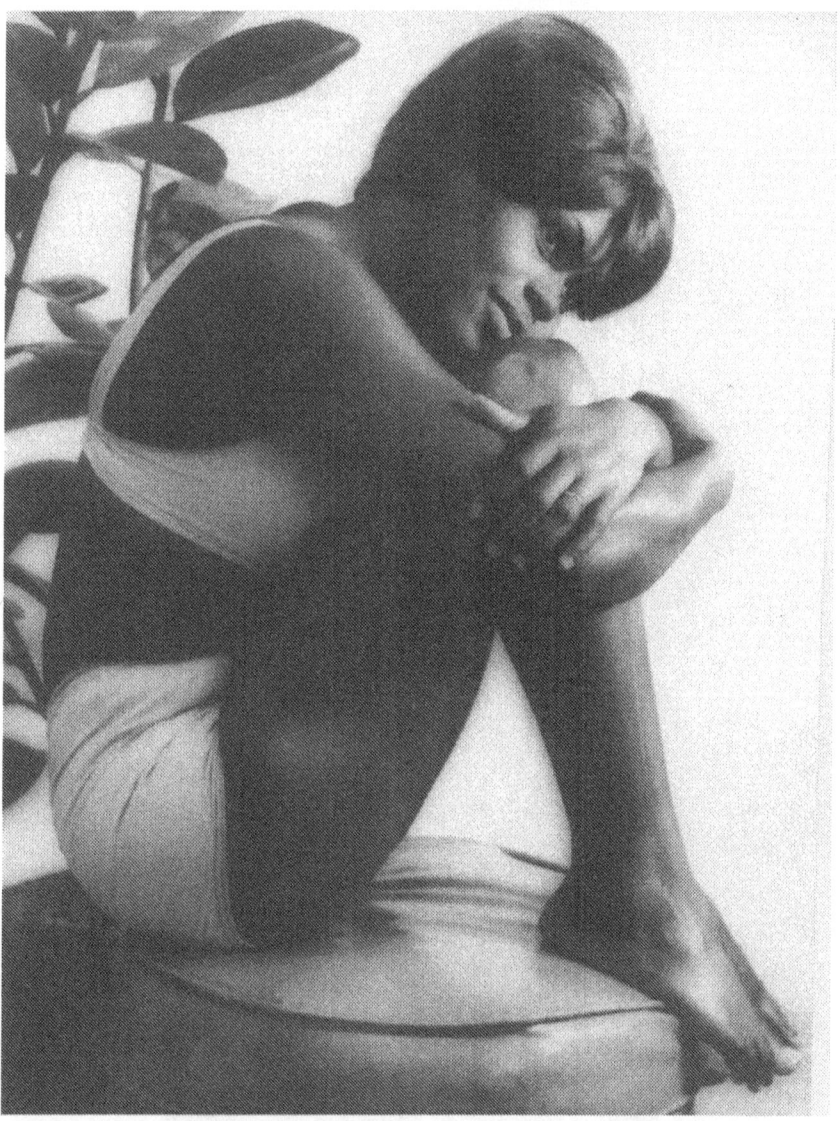

*Mary Taylor-Langford 3ʳᵈ Place Winner in American Bandstand's
Bathing Suit Beauty Contest with Dick Clark in 1966*

Leah Lewis-Taylor's Brother-Cicero Lewis

Leah Lewis-Taylor's Sister Emma Lewis-Howell

Leah Lewis-Taylor's Nephew Freddie Mack Lewis

About the Author

Mary Taylor-Langford is the author of Mister Buddha. A true story about the Langford family's incredible bond with "man's best friend," a wonderful dog they named Buddha.

She is a graduate of Bishop College and the University of Massachusetts at Amherst, MA with a Master's Degree in Education and has worked in the Human Service field for over 25 years, She is married to Harold F. Langford, Jr. and is the mother of three: Harold, III, Charles, and Virna. She is retired from the Commonwealth of Massachusetts—Department of Social Services. She resides in New England with her husband.

www.ingramcontent.com/pod-product-compliance
Lightning Source LLC
Chambersburg PA
CBHW031242280526
45784CB00004B/1685